Lean Recruitment (Effective Recruiting Strategy)

By Ade Asefeso MCIPS MBA

Copyright 2018 by Ade Asefeso MCIPS MBA
All rights reserved.

First Edition

ISBN-13: 978-1986174336

ISBN-10: 1986174336

Publisher: AA Global Sourcing Ltd
Website: http://www.aaglobalsourcing.com

Table of Contents

Disclaimer 5
Dedication 6
Chapter 1: Introduction 7
Chapter 2: Lean Just-in-Time Recruiting 13
Chapter 3: How to Apply Lean Principles in Recruiting 25
Chapter 4: Applying the Principles of Lean Manufacturing to Recruiting 29
Chapter 5: Use Lean to Do More with Less 35
Chapter 6: Benefits of Just-In-Time Recruiting 41
Chapter 7: Get on Board with Just-in-Time Recruiting 47
Chapter 8: Human Capital Supply Chain Management Recruiting 51
Chapter 9: Think Outside the Box 55
Chapter 10: Tips to Improve Your Talent Acquisition 59
Chapter 11: High Performing Talent Acquisition Function 63
Chapter 12: Testing Cultural Fit During the Recruitment Process 67
Chapter 13: Recruiting for Fit Instead of Experience and Education 71
Chapter 14: Effective Small Business Recruitment 75
Chapter 15: Big Business Recruitment Strategy 79

Chapter 16: Ways to Attract Top Millennial Talent 83
Chapter 17: Need for Speed in Recuitment is Increasing 87
Chapter 18: Why Speed Matters in Recruitment ... 93
Chapter 19: The Process of Recruiting Faster 97
Chapter 20: Strategies to Attracting Passive Talents 101
Chapter 21: Argument for Effective Employee Referral Program 109
Chapter 22: Guide to Building the Perfect Employee Referral Program 115
Chapter 23: Effective Engagement and Referral Tactics and Strategies 125
Chapter 24: Conclusion 133

Disclaimer

This publication is designed to provide competent and reliable information regarding the subject matter covered. However, it is sold with the understanding that the author and publisher are not engaged in rendering professional advice. The authors and publishers specifically disclaim any liability that is incurred from the use or application of contents of this book.

If you purchased this book without a cover you should be aware that this book may have been stolen property and reported as "unsold and destroyed" to the publisher. In this case neither the author nor the publisher has received any payment for this "stripped book."

Dedication

To those who will never settle for less than they can be.

To my family and friends who seems to have been sent here to teach me something about who I am supposed to be. They have nurtured me, challenged me, and even opposed me.... But at every juncture has taught me!

The future has many names. For the weak, it's unattainable. For the fearful, it's unknown. For the bold, it's ideal.

Remember whether you think you can, or you think you cannot you will bee right.

Chapter 1: Introduction

What does the phrase "lean recruiting" bring to mind?

A small talent acquisition team making the most of a limited budget?

Bare bones recruitment methods?

Lean recruiting has been adapted from the concept of lean manufacturing, and it continuously improves the talent acquisition process by eliminating waste and increasing efficiency.

Why exactly should recruiters focus on this continuous improvement method?

We often discuss the importance of developing consumer-quality career sites, and building talent pipelines. These strategies take time and resources. Should talent acquisition leaders also continuously monitor these efforts, and terminate with indifference those variables that are consistently inefficient?

Sort of; recruitment strategies should not be implemented and then unceremoniously tossed out the window; but Human Resources "HR" leaders should be fully prepared to review their efforts, acknowledge processes that are wasteful and unproductive, and make serious changes or adaptations in response.

In this chapter we will explain the concept of lean recruiting, and highlight three takeaways for your talent acquisition strategy. This chapter is not intended to inspire you to completely change your strategy and start practicing "lean recruiting" tomorrow; it's meant to make you think of recruiting process improvements from a different angle.

So what is Lean Recruiting?

Lean manufacturing is a method for eliminating waste within manufacturing processes. Famously developed by Toyota as the Toyota Production System (TPS) in the mid-1900s, some refer to this system as "just-in-time" production. By reviewing and changing the manufacturing process to remove inconsistent and overburdened workloads, waste is reduced.

Toyota's approach led to more flexible and adaptive manufacturing systems, focused on the value that customers are willing to pay for. Talent acquisition leaders who see the global talent war as really a competition over supply chain management can see the parallels here between manufacturing and recruitment.

Typical supply chains transfer raw goods through the manufacturing process and end with finished products a customer can buy. The human capital supply chain takes relationships and recruitment data and transforms that into candidates hiring managers can choose from. Looking at the process on its most basic level, recruiters move something of value (people) from a source to the consumer (employers).

So lean recruiting reviews the talent acquisition process as a whole, identifies wasteful and inefficient components, and eliminates or replaces them. This makes the overall system of identifying, acquiring and retaining candidates a better human capital supply chain.

But how exactly can recruiters implement these ideas into their talent acquisition strategy?

1. Strong Metrics and Talent Acquisition Strategy.

Lean recruitment starts with looking at your entire talent acquisition strategy. What are the different processes involved in filling an open position? How are those processes tracked or measured? As we mentioned in the beginning of this chapter, it's not enough to build your system and let it run as is. Your recruitment methods need to be analyzed, adapted, sometimes changed entirely, to remain cost-effective and successful.

So the first step towards lean recruiting is the establishment of your talent acquisition strategy, and determining the metrics you will use to monitor its success. The uptake of data and the reduction of waste is more important than ever in recruitment. By approaching talent acquisition from the position of increasing efficiency and customer satisfaction, Human Resources "HR" leaders can better demonstrate not just the importance of their work, but also its results and the notion of eliminating waste should already be top of mind as you implement your recruitment methods and track their results. Some of the big sources of waste in lean manufacturing include overproduction and over processing. In lean recruiting, running too many processes to source candidates, and analyzing too much data, is more likely to hinder your results than improve them.

2. Recruitment Metrics and Strategy Review.

You have developed a talent acquisition strategy, distributed the responsibilities among your team, and now you can sit back and watch the quality candidates roll in, right?

Sure, if you want to watch your competitors hire the best and brightest while you are left scratching your head.

Lean recruiting at this stage means reviewing every component of your talent acquisition methods and identifying areas for improvement. We already mentioned two important sources of waste in your human capital supply chain. Now it's time to look for defective production, motion, and waiting.

Waste from defects is pretty simple; something isn't working as it should, and your team wastes time and resources finding and fixing the problems. This can lead to both motion (people and resources in action more than is required) and waiting (interruptions to the system while waiting for one process).

Is one of your job boards expensive, but consistently returning sub-par candidates?

Does your team spend too much time analyzing every data point?

Are managers kept waiting too long before they can interview quality candidates?

These are just a few examples of the waste that can arise. Taking a serious look at your processes will help you eliminate inefficiencies and adapt to changing trends.

3. Continuous Improvement Based on Results.

So you have established your recruitment strategy and the metrics you will use to measure its success. You have reviewed the whole system and found some genuine room for improvement. How do you move forward?

Change is hard, but if you can accept that not everything will work perfectly the first time, you will end up with a much more flexible talent acquisition strategy.

Inventory is an important source of waste to consider here. Perhaps your team has spent a lot of time building up a talent pipeline; but when an opening actually arises, most of those candidates have already found other jobs, or they are content where they are.

Was it worth your time to develop the talent pipeline?

Some Human Resources "HR" leaders say no, or at least that talent pipelines are leaky and inefficient if built incorrectly. They point out that in IT, some managers bypass Human Resources "HR" and source their own candidates; much in the same way they use agile software development to continuously improve their products. If your own colleagues are ignoring your efforts to hire employees, it's time to adapt your strategy. Let your ability to strategize, execute, and adapt based on the results demonstrate the true value of your talent acquisition team.

Chapter 2: Lean Just-in-Time Recruiting

We cannot talk about Lean without Just-in-Time. The process of identifying an organization's talent needs and identifying, acquiring, and retaining talent for those needs is essentially human capital supply chain management.

A supply chain is a system of organizations, people, technology, activities, information and resources involved in moving something of value (a product, a service, or a person) from a source to a customer or consumer.

Conventional supply chain activities transform natural resources, raw materials and components into a finished product that is delivered to the end customer.

In recruiting, human capital supply chain activities transform relationships and data (ad responses, resumes, social networking profiles, etc.) into candidates that are delivered to hiring managers.

So why is it that there is quite a bit of resistance to applying proven supply chain management principles and practices to human resources and recruiting functions?

We will be looking at Lean principles and Just-in-Time concepts that can and should be applied to recruiting in this chapter; because Lean has been highly refined by Toyota, many people associate Lean almost exclusively with manufacturing; however, Lean principles can and have been applied to a wide variety of non-manufacturing processes and organizations, including services and many others as demonstrated in our other Lean books. What I find especially interesting is that many companies have been applying Lean and continuous improvement principles to various parts of their organization for years, but very few think to apply them to their human resources and recruiting organizations. I hope to change that with this book.

The primary focus of Lean is creating more value with less work, and considers the expenditure of resources for any goal other than the creation of value for the end customers.

Would your customers (candidates, employees and hiring managers) have any issues with you focusing primarily on creating value for them? I didn't think so.

Activities that don't add value or are unproductive are wasteful (Muda is the Japanese term for waste).

Critical to effectively leveraging Lean is the identification of which steps in a process add value to customers and which do not. After classifying process activities into these two categories, the focus is to take steps to improve the former and eliminate the latter.

Having a good understanding of the hidden wastes inside of the recruiting process will aid in your appreciation of what Just-In-Time recruiting is designed to accomplish.

If it Doesn't Add Value – it's Waste!

In Lean recruiting, anything that does not provide value to candidates, employees, and hiring managers is waste.

There are 7 wastes identified by Lean and I think that overproduction, inventory, defects, over-processing, and waiting are among the most rampant in recruiting.

1. Overproduction

Overproduction is production ahead of and in excess of demand.

In sourcing and recruiting, overproduction happens every time you attract, identify and engage more candidates than needed to deliver to your customer. Traditional proactive candidate pipelining ahead of actual hiring need almost always leads to overproduction.

You have never looked at proactive candidate pipelining this way have you?

Posting jobs online also leads to overproduction, because more people apply than can be realistically processed. Many companies don't even attempt to respond to all applicants, while others will send an automated reply. If you get so many responses that you can't reply to them all or have to resort to auto-responders, isn't that a clue that it is a wasteful process?

Inventory

In recruiting, your candidate pipeline is your inventory. More specifically your work-in-process candidate inventory.

Work-in-process is a production/supply chain concept, used to describe "unfinished" inventory in a production process; this inventory is "either just being fabricated or waiting in a queue for further processing or in a buffer storage."

A group of candidates that a recruiter stays in routine contact to maintain a relationship with, without a specific and current hiring need is essentially a work-in-process candidate inventory.

When most recruiters talk about proactively pipelining candidates; they are really referring to building work-in-process candidate inventories. Candidates in a work-in-process pipeline are typically people identified by a resourcer or a recruiter as people whose work history/experience somewhat closely matches the kinds of positions that an organization typically recruits for. Once identified, these candidates are contacted and screened (to some extent).

These are candidates that are waiting on further "processing" (interviewing, networking, etc.), and the vast majority remain permanently "in process." In other words, a relationship is maintained with them indefinitely, as the vast majority of these candidates never become a "finished product" (are never hired).

Candidates in a work-in-process pipeline may be active, passive, or not even looking, and may or may not precisely fit any current hiring needs; however, time and effort is expended to build and maintain a relationship with these candidates to be ready when an opening does arise, or when the candidate's situation changes and they become available, or to simply network with to gain intelligent and referrals.

Lean thinking would tell us that the time and effort expended to maintain a work-in-process inventory of pipelined candidates is pure waste.

Sitting indefinitely in the "relationship maintenance" phase doesn't provide any real value for the candidates or clients.

Let's not pretend we don't know what happens to those candidates when the positions you pipelined them forget filled by other candidates, never get approved or never become available. We are all also painfully aware of the perishable nature of work-in-process candidate inventory. People do not remain "recruitable" indefinitely; everyone has a shelf life. As such, recruiters are constantly trying to keep their candidate inventory fresh (finding new people to pipeline, maintaining contact with everyone to see if they are still available, etc.) because good candidates are perishable; they don't stay ripe for recruiting long.

2. Defects

According to Lean, a "defect" is something that does not conform to specifications or expectations.

When it comes to recruiting, I am not suggesting that the people themselves are defects; however, candidates that are sourced, contacted, screened, and with whom a relationship is maintained that do not ultimately match the actual hiring need are defects of the recruiting process.

Defects arise whenever job specifications and requirements change from forecast, rendering pipelined candidates no longer qualified, or when candidates are no longer interested, available, or when their motivators change away from your opportunity. Forecasts are never perfect; they can't be. Positions and requirements change, and people don't stay interested or available forever.

A large number of defects are caused by posting jobs online.

Yes, I know you probably think I am crazy to question job posting; but it is the dirty little secret of recruiting and it is a global phenomenon.

We all know that a huge percentage of people who respond to jobs online do not meet the basic qualifications of the positions they are applying for. The fact is, posting jobs results in a very high number of defects applicants who do not meet the basic qualifications.

3. Over-processing

Over-processing occurs any time more work is done than what is required by the customer.

Engaging, screening and building and maintaining relationships with candidates that will never ultimately be submitted to a client/manager in consideration for an interview can be seen as performing more work than necessary and be classified as over-processing.

Your hiring managers don't actually require you to maintain relationships with a large number of people who will likely no longer be available or interested or even qualified when you actually have a need.

What value do these candidates ever provide to hiring managers?

I don't know any active or passive job seeker that actually wants to have you contact, engage, and maintain relationships with them if you will never actually submit them in consideration for a position they did be interested in accepting an offer for.

4. Waiting

Lean defines the waste of waiting as any time that something is held in wait of the next production step.

In recruiting, waiting occurs whenever candidates are not being advanced through the recruiting and hiring process.

In most recruiting processes, a large part of a candidate's life is spent waiting to be moved forward in the process. Most candidates that respond to a job posting or are contacted by a recruiter are never advanced past an automated response (at worst) or the relationship maintenance phase (at best).

Any candidate that doesn't actually progress through the hiring process (at least to an interview with the hiring manager/team) is essentially stuck in a permanent holding pattern; indefinitely waiting.

Maintaining relationships with candidates is not moving forward it's a holding pattern, which for many candidates, is permanent.

One May Ask; what is Just-In-Time Recruiting?

Now that you have a good understanding of what Lean is all about (providing value to customers and reducing waste), let's focus on the concept of Just-In-Time.

Just-In-Time (JIT) production is a pull-based production strategy that is also called the Toyota Production System.

A critical Lean concept, Just-In-Time strives to enable companies to react to specific demands with agility and speed with the goal of producing the exact product (or performing the exact service) that a customer wants, when they want it, in the amount they want.

Applying this concept to talent identification and acquisition, Just-In-Time recruiting is a pull-based strategy of providing hiring managers/clients with candidates that exactly match their needs, when they want them, in the amount they want.

Just-In-Time strategy is designed specifically to reduce the wastes of overproduction, inventory, defects, over-processing, and waiting. Instead of proactively building and maintaining work-in-process candidate pipelines without an actual hiring need (a push-based strategy), Just-In-Time recruiting has a primary focus of tapping into "raw material" candidate inventory (resumes, LinkedIn profiles, your network, etc.) and contacting, qualifying, and delivering candidates only in direct response to a hiring need.

A fundamental principle of Lean is demand-based flow production. In this type of production setting, inventory is only pulled through each production centre when it is needed to meet a customer's order. In Just-In-Time recruiting, recruiters only contact, screen and submit candidates in response to a client's (internal or external) "order" these processed candidates are pulled through the recruiting lifecycle based on actual demand.

When properly executed, a recruiter can source, contact, screen/interview candidates and submit the best to a hiring authority for consideration within 24-48 hours of being given the "green light" for a specific position; all without having a traditional pipeline of candidates that have been "kept warm."

Yes, even for very rare hiring profiles.

I am sure that for many of you, It seem crazy for applying Lean principles, the Toyota Production System, and Just-In-Time to sourcing and recruiting processes and organizations.

To convince you of my sanity (and that I am on to something here), it may help for you to know that I am not writing in theory, but from practical experience in applying these principles that goes back to 2006.

I did not read a bunch of books and try to adapt Lean and Just-In-Time production to recruiting. Practically everything I write about comes directly from experiences of one of the top recruiters I interviewed and shadowed since 2006. She said "during my early years in the recruiting industry, in the trenches, working a recruiting desk in a highly competitive recruiting agency, 8 years before I even heard of the concepts of Just-In-Time and Lean. What I learned largely through my own trial and error in the process of trying to not only keep my new job but also become the top performer for the company ended up being uncannily aligned with core Lean and Just-In-Time philosophy; creating more value for my candidates and clients with less work, giving them exactly what they want, when they want it, and reducing the wastes of overproduction, inventory, defects, over-processing, and waiting."

I think it is critical to constantly question status quo and to always be looking to innovate and improve.

The desire to keep doing things the way you have been taught, and "the way they have always been done" can be considered as evidence of the desire to remain comfortable.

I am asking you to step outside of your zone of competence (and comfort!) and explore Lean principles and Just-In-Time methodology. I am challenging you to spend more than just a few minutes to examine your recruiting processes and organization with a critical eye for creating more value for your candidates and your hiring managers, and to identify waste, such as unnecessary work in progress candidate inventory, over-processing, excessive waiting, overproduction, and defects.

Many companies talk a good game about innovation, but in my opinion, I think one of the last areas in every company to focus on innovation is human resources and recruiting. This is totally backwards if you really think about it. The people you hire are the ones who create new products and services and find new and innovative ways of doing business.

Being more innovative in sourcing and recruiting can give you a sustainable competitive advantage by enabling you to find and hire more of the right people who can drive innovation throughout your entire organisation.

Chapter 3: How to Apply Lean Principles in Recruiting

As stated before in this book Lean (or kaizen, continuous improvement) is not a new term in manufacturing, but it is not limited to production as many people think. Let's see how recruiters can adopt lean principles to reduce wastes and enhance process efficiency.

The focus of lean is doing more with less. It seems to be the ultimate objective of any process in the world. The main principles of lean are creating and adding more values for customers by reducing waste in processes. Here are some key factors to remember:

1. Continuous improvement
2. Waste elimination
3. Customer centralization
4. Just-in-time operation
5. Employee empowerment

Since lean has been practiced in manufacturing industry for dedicates, many people think that it belongs to production only. Yet these principles of continuous improvement can be applied to every process in any business to gain the best efficiency.

For Human Resources in general and recruiting in particular, lean can help the whole organization save cost, time and effort while improve the quality.

Customers of recruitment processes are organization, divisions, departments, teams (current employees) and potential candidates, of course. Lean recruiting aims to add more values for these end users and let them be the drivers of continuous change and improvement. Thus, as a recruiter, you need to understand the needs of every single work groups and take feedback regularly for the best results. In the long run, recruitment team in particular and Human Resources department in general need to create and develop a lean culture in the whole organization.

Anything that doesn't create values to customers and stakeholders is called waste. In recruiting, we usually think that the costs are external expenditure on hiring, but it's not so simple. Although time to fill a vacancy is considered as one of top three valuable metrics of recruiting team performance in the LinkedIn Global Recruiting Trends 2016, not many hiring managers talk about hidden cost under long time of hire.

Waste occurs on every day practices of hiring teams in sourcing, screening, interviewing and so on. By doing repetitively the same tasks every work day during the recruiting time, recruiters can only create a little real values. In a worse case, a wrong hiring decision can cost more than you imagine.

Below are some suggestions.

Create standard frameworks and procedures
These materials will be used for automation (screening software, repetitive processes, etc). You

can quickly shortlist candidates who meet minimum requirements with less effort than ever.

Make use of employee referral program

Not by chance is employee referral program a top source of quality of hire for several years (Source: LinkedIn Global Recruiting Trends 2014, 2015, 2016). When recruiting a referral candidate, both recruiter and job seeker can benefit from less time, money and effort wasted. These sources of candidates often have better performance, productivity and longer tenure as well. We look into this deeply later in this book.

Understand the variability to adapt to any change

There are some times that your company needs to hire massive positions while some other times there is no demand at all. You need to analyze data of your company as well as the industry in several years to predict the needs and demands for different periods. By this way, you can quickly reallocate resources and handle all changes well.

Empower employees for the best innovation results

Employee empowerment is not about managing people. Lean leaders need to encourage employees to think, act, react and control their own work. Please avoid micro managing style in a lean culture. Let all recruiting team members be the masters of their process, and resolve their problems by themselves in an autonomous way. It is the fastest and most effective approach for continuous improvement.

Take feedback from stakeholders during hiring process

It is the base for continuously improvement in recruitment process. As a hiring manager, you need to take candidate experience into account in every single step of recruitment. Also, keeping connected with other departments will help you take timely actions to provide the best values for the whole organization.

Chapter 4: Applying the Principles of Lean Manufacturing to Recruiting

Lean manufacturing has been a regular practice in Japan for over 50 years, where it has helped Toyota achieve high profits and a breakeven point in car manufacturing way below that of competitors. Many American and European manufacturers have adopted the techniques of lean manufacturing as well, and have used it to keep costs down, to improve productivity, and even to reduce the need to hire more employees.

There is nothing difficult to understand about the concepts of lean manufacturing. It is usually defined as a systematic approach to identifying and then eliminating any waste in a process.

Waste is defined as a non-value-added activity. Conversely, it is about improving efficiency and customer satisfaction. It also contains the important concept of continuous improvement and letting the customer be the driver of change. In other words, as customer tastes and requirements change, the process should adapt to those new requirements easily. While I am not going to discuss lean manufacturing in this book, I am going to try and show how the same principles can be applied to any process, such as recruiting. I have called it "lean process improvement" (LPI). There are four principles that are at the core of lean process improvement as it applies to recruiting:

1. The rigorous hunt for waste (activities that do not directly interface with a candidate or hiring manager) and its elimination.

2. An effort to understand what causes change or variability in the recruiting process, and to apply techniques to either eliminate the variability or adapt to it.

3. The ability to streamline processes and use technology to cope with the ever-changing environment.

4. To fully appreciate the value of recruiters and make sure they are being used to their best ability.

Let's look at each of these in greater detail.

Waste Elimination Recruiting: Is a wasteful process as it is normally practiced today. There are many non-value-added activities, including everything that has to do with handling electronic or paper data, all scheduling and report writing, and much of both the candidate and the hiring manager interface. Take a normal recruiting day. A recruiter may start her day by looking at email and at the (probably) hundreds of resumes or electronic profiles that have accumulated overnight for the positions that recruiter has open. A half-day or more may be taken up simply scanning and screening these emails and resumes/CV, with no decisions being made and with no candidate contact. The rest of the day may be taken up with phone screens for the few good candidates, many of whom will turn out to be not so good, or in chats with hiring managers updating them on progress or querying them about the skills or background of a particular candidate.

There may be an interview or two somewhere in this mix or even the need to go meet a new hiring manager and determine the requirements for a new position. Out of all of these activities only a small percentage is value-added. Determining what adds value is one of the most challenging aspects of lean process improvement. Adding value in recruiting would be whenever you are talking directly with a candidate to either determine their skills or to convince them to join your organization. It is also whenever you are directly in conversation with a hiring manager about a candidate or a position. Value-added is when you are networking with potential candidates, communicating with candidates, or working on the front-end of the recruiting process.

Waste occurs when you are doing data entry, filing, database searching, resume review, scheduling, and even some levels of interviewing where you are not a decision maker. Waste also occurs when you have steps in your process that are redundant or unnecessary. Lean processes are efficient, which means they use the smallest amount of time and resources possible. Recruiting processes are filled with steps that do not necessarily lead to better or faster decisions. Some steps are required by law or corporate policy, but many can be eliminated or shortened.

The focus should be on determining what the best theoretical cycle time would be or the minimum amount of time it would take for the perfect candidate to be identified and hired. If, for example, it were possible to identify and hire a person for a particular position in two days given that everything went smoothly, all interviews took place efficiently, and so on, then that would be the cycle time you should aim to achieve on a regular basis. You can then work backwards and eliminate or reduce all the things that get in the way of achieving that.

Understanding Variability Recruiting is often cyclical: There are times when demand for candidates is so high that every recruiter is frustrated and other times when not much is going on. This is true of many functions, and one of the key lessons of lean process improvement is to understand and level out these cycles or adapt to them. One method is to use historical patterns to predict variability. It is common for organizations to have seasons when recruiting is very slow and others when things tend to pick up.

The retail world can safely predict a hiring "binge" every November and December as holiday sales increase. By using technology well, using resources in multiple ways, and by being able to quickly reallocate resources, it is possible to smooth out this variability and maintain low recruiter headcounts while still handing a high volume of candidates. Most recruiters could handle significant increases in candidate loads if they used technology better and eliminated waste as we have defined it.

Remain Adaptable by Improving Processes and Applying Technology: Being able to adapt to ever changing customer demands and expectations of both those of candidates and of hiring mangers is a skill we will all need in increasing amounts as we move into a renewed economy. Technology can help at every step.

The web can brand your organization, it can persuade and sell the organization to candidates, and it can screen candidates to a level where an investment of the recruiter's time makes sense. Technology can automate the scheduling and backend processes that are so wasteful in recruiting and it can give the recruiter the freedom to be adaptable and move to areas that need attention while not being swamped with other activities.

Most recruiting functions could find many steps in their recruiting processes that could be eliminated and procedures that could be streamlined or automated by the use of technology. While manufacturing has applied technology widely to reduce the number of workers and to improve speed and quality, we are just starting to think about this in recruiting. There is a lot of low hanging fruit. I believe an average recruiting function could improve its capacity by twofold as well as its candidate quality, with a very tiny amount of technology and process improvement.

Use People Well: This brings us to the way skilled recruiters are being used today; as often as little more than clerks. Many are processing electronic or paper data, endlessly phone screening candidates that are not really qualified, and fighting internal battles with other departments or with internal policy and bureaucracy. Often they end up spending less than half of their time directly in contact with a candidate. While recruiters need to develop a multiple set of skills that add value, they also need processes improved to allow them to use those skills.

One of the keys to lean process improvement is to use people where they perform best. This means that recruiters need to be freed to apply their people skills and how well and how much time they spend doing this should be how they are rewarded. Understanding the power of lean process improvement and then applying it to your recruiting function can make you much more effective and can improve candidate and hiring manager satisfaction.

Chapter 5: Use Lean to Do More with Less.

Lean is a principle we have adapted with great success within our own business and has formed the basis of recommendations to our clients to maximise efficiencies and streamline processes within their recruitment process. This chapter outlines how you might use lean to do more with less within your recruitment process.

Just to remind ourselves again the core idea of Lean is to maximize customer value while minimizing waste. Simply, lean means creating more value for customers with fewer resources.

Let's look at how you can streamline your recruitment processes by accommodating lean thinking into your recruitment process.

1. Customer Focused

Toyota strategists understood that, in order to adopt a process that eliminated waste and increased value adding processes, they needed to look at things from a consumer-centric standpoint. Only then could they really identify the areas that were adding value.

In the recruitment industry, this equates to understanding the needs of the various customers in your business, whether they are individuals, departments, teams, divisions, candidates or clients.

Each group must be assessed separately, analysing data (where possible), to ascertain what makes their lives easier and their recruitment journeys efficient and stress free. This can be achieved through regular feedback from clients, candidates and your consultants themselves.

2. Identifying and Eliminating Waste

There is a suggestion that, for most manufacturing operations, "only 5% of activities actually add value, 35% are necessary non value adding activities and 60% add no value at all." In short, if a process adds no value to the customer then it is waste.

Looking at those figures, anyone in a position of seniority in a recruitment business that seeks to improve the bottom line must ask two critical questions:

    a. What percentage of your processes really adds value to your customer?
    b. What activities can be made more efficient?

These simple questions often result in uncomfortable answers.

For example, the time to fill a vacancy is a valuable metric which can suffer because of waste occurring in everyday routines through each step of the recruitment journey; from sourcing the right candidate, screening and interviewing, to placement. With each step, waste can be identified and by adopting lean thinking gradually, you can begin to streamline each procedure.

There are often massive room for improvement, but a few simple building blocks will help you start to eliminate waste:

   a. Ensure processes are followed during the candidate acquisition, registration and interview process.
   b. Create standardised procedures for screening and registering candidates.
   c. Identify what data needs to be captured and entered in your recruitment software at each stage of the recruitment process.
   d. Continually review the way data is entered, managed and searched for in your recruitment software.
   e. Record and review where you placed candidates are sourced from.
   f. Map the candidate journey from CV collection to placement, and understand how technology can be used to automate repetitive tasks, track the candidate journey and reduce errors from double keying data.

By analysing individual processes and identifying where the value really lies, your frontline staff can recruit more efficiently and spend more time undertaking value adding activities.

Under the leadership of Taiichi Ohno, Toyota implemented a significant move away from the manufacturing norm to the Just in Time (JIT) process where parts were supplied only as and when they were required; although this process left, "no room for error," its success was undeniable and became widely accepted by other global organisations. In a study, American and European firms that introduced just-in-time achieved an average 50% reduction in labour costs and 70% reduction in inventory over 4 years.

The theory behind this revolutionary framework can, also, be adopted to streamline your recruitment processes. By analysing and relying on the quality of your data and identifying trends in the market and your business, you can predict which candidates need to be supplied just at the point where the demand is rising allowing your consultants to source the highest quality candidates before demand peaks; however, this can only be effective with a lean recruitment database and rigorous processes in place.

Another example of where just-in-time can eliminate waste is in candidate compliance.

So much time is wasted getting every candidate compliant as quickly as possible. By applying the just-in-time philosophy, you can focus on supplying compliant candidates as and when they are needed. For example, from your data you may know that your clients in Norwich need 30% more carer workers in December. This enables you to prepare more candidates and ensure they are compliant, ready for the increased demand.

3. Employee Empowerment

The communication and trust required to ensure lean thinking can operate at its peak begins with every employee. Their endorsement of the philosophy is as important as the moving parts in Toyota's manufacturing line. The clear frameworks and structural foundations should negate the need for micromanagement and empower your employees.

For example, train and allow employees to deal with issues autonomously (have an escalation process where needed) and have a feedback process for improvements. Employees should feel determined and empowered to analyse and improve your processes with you. An empowered workforce is the most efficient route to continuous improvement.

4. Continuous Improvement

Every successful process needs to be reviewed and tweaked because every business will have their own specific requirements and methods for reducing waste. By analysing your recorded data and listening to your employees and customers, you can refine your processes and implement a more streamlined and efficient strategy that is bespoke to your business.

Chapter 6: Benefits of Just-In-Time Recruiting

With the growth of just-in-time recruiting, Human Resources leaders can now consider the spectrum of how work is getting done in modern businesses. In particular, many organizations are benefiting from the flexibility and value of just-in-time recruiting.

The truth about talent acquisition is that many businesses limit their own options by holding rigid views on recruiting. We tend to think in terms of our existing processes and categories. If our business operations are arranged to categorize every talent resource as either full-time or part-time, and as either salaried or contract, we may overlook other recruiting options.

Building a talent pipeline does not have to depend on black-and-white choices between creating new positions and negotiating one-off contracts with freelancers. In particular, many organizations are benefiting from the flexibility and value of just-in-time recruiting.

As we discussed before in this book; businesses are beginning to take queues from just-in-time manufacturing and just-in-time inventory. With this lean methodology, companies are reaping huge rewards for using just-in-time recruiting to fill their teams. Some of the major benefits these companies are seeing includes.

1. **Efficiency**

Just-in-time is a "pull system", which means that new labour is only pulled into the team if the demand for it exists. It lets companies fill the gaps on their staffs without producing organizational excess.

From a business perspective, this helps companies become much leaner, removing redundancies from their processes and lowering labour costs simultaneously.

2. **Speed**

Just-in-time recruiting moves fast. That is the advantage of letting a dedicated agency find and recruit your talent for you instead of delegating the task to your Human Resources Department, which has plenty of other obligations to attend to.

It is common for agencies to "source, contact, screen/interview candidates and submit the best within 24 - 48 hours". If a sudden need arises, you can rely on agency like Spring Raise Ltd to get someone at the door quickly.

3. **Risk Reduction**

Despite your efforts on a traditional hiring process, sometimes a new hire doesn't pay off; a worker can turn out to be a poor fit for your company for any number of reasons. Replacing an employee, however, is costly. It takes time and money to recruit a new candidate, and unfilled positions result in lost productivity.

By contrast, just-in-time workers are easy to replace. The agency handles it for you, and quickly. The stakes involved in bringing a new person on the team are lowered, making recruitment a less risky endeavour.

4. Agility

Furthermore, when you are unencumbered by the logistical responsibilities of hiring employees, you can change the shape of your staff more easily to suit your needs at that exact moment. Example: A lot of companies feel obligated to have fully-staffed engineering departments because they want to have people on hand when major development projects come up. When dry spells come and software engineers are less able to contribute.

But with just-in-time recruitment, you can simply bring on development professionals whenever there is a need, and release them when that work is completed. It is a dynamic recruiting approach for times that fit with the dynamic solutions that modern technology companies are trying to provide.

The Flipside

While just-in-time recruiting makes it much easier to procure talent, customary management methods aren't always suited to this model. You may have to make adjustments if you want to help this part of your team to achieve their best.

1. Training

Companies want their just-in-timers to be up and working as soon as possible, but some degree of training is necessary for them to function on your team.

You cannot just use the same standard training you use for your employees; much of it may not relate to short-term roles and you should not use stock courses, which won't reflect your company's values or employer brand, either.

So what do you do?

Simple: just follow the just-in-time model. Create unique training content for the unique needs of your just-in-time workers. Course authoring tools will let you make small, impactful, personalized courses that provide just-in-time trainees with everything they need to get started; no more, no less.

Also, try building training directly into your workflows by giving people a course to accompany them when learning something complex for the first time; like operating a piece of complex machinery or navigating your contact management system can boost their time-to-competency and retention.

2. Integration

Getting short-term employees to collaborate with your staff's regulars can be tricky. One issue is that because their employment situation is different, they may feel excluded from discussions of important issues or from critical communication.

To allay these feelings of exclusion, give just-in-time workers a proper welcome. That may be small gestures like a note at their cubicle or inviting them to a team lunch. It definitely includes reviewing all the tools and platforms they will need to connect with the rest of the team.

3. Engagement

It doesn't matter if someone works for you full-time or is only on for a week; engagement is a management priority. Unfortunately, because of their unique situation, it can be tougher to engage just-in-time employees. Knowing that their employment is fixed and short-term, some temps are focused on finding their next job or worrying about second jobs to go to after they leave your office.

Since you can't get the best out of a worker if you don't have their full attention, you need to make sure just-in-time roles are engrossing and interesting.

Consider these three ways to do this:

    a. Provide training that teaches them new, valuable skills.
    a. Seek their input in your decision-making process.
    b. Ensure they have an understanding of the project's objectives and of their role in it.

A Savvier Recruiting Solution

Despite the learning curve involved in managing the just-in-time workforce, this approach to recruiting is still enormously beneficial. The savings, efficiencies, and leanness more than make up for the small accommodations you will need to make.

The next time you find yourself in that awkward space between having too much work for your team but not enough to justify hiring another person, remember that there is another, better option besides asking people to work overtime. By making smart use of just-in-time staff and taking small tactical steps to keep them onboard and engaged; you can get just what you need.

Chapter 7: Get on Board with Just-in-Time Recruiting

In the Human Resources world of business recruiting; whether you are working for a recruiting agency or a private company; finding the best candidates exactly when you need them is rarely simple. More often than not, the hiring process is muddled by an overwhelming number of less-than-qualified candidates for the position you need filled, along with a small number of qualified candidates who are not really available or interested.

The traditional recruiting approach has been to develop a talent pipeline as a way of cultivating potential candidates for future employment opportunities, by building and maintaining relationships with a number of desirable applicants. The idea is that when an opportunity becomes available, you will have a number of people you can approach who have already warmed up to your company. Unfortunately this method tends to be wasteful and ineffective.

Why is the traditional talent pipeline method no longer the best approach? Let's take a closer look.

Over-processing: They say time is money, so you don't want to waste it. When you spend time cultivating potential candidates who may or may not be interested in a job that may or may not come up, you are wasting time. You are spending time building relationships with people who may not be available, interested, or qualified for an opportunity when it comes up. In any case, you are making more work for yourself by cultivating relationships that most likely won't come to fruition.

Unused inventory: Talent pipelines can also be wasteful in terms of the number of candidates you have amassed. Do your contacts in "relationship maintenance mode" help you hire smarter and/or do they help your company's bottom line? Chances are they don't. Toyota Motor Company originally came up with the idea that inventory equals waste. It affects a company's efficiency and profitability, and diverts resources from where they can be better used. To avoid having any inventory, Toyota came up with the Just-In-Time method of production.

Lack of quality: Say you have spent months, maybe years, developing a traditional talent pipeline, and now finally a position that must be filled immediately opens up. You turn to your pool of candidates and find… what? Chances are your talent pool is filled to the brim with candidates, but are any of them the one? It may even be that you have scoped out a candidate in your pool who did be perfect for a certain position; however, by the time the position opens up, the position requirements have shifted because company priorities have changed, so the candidate is no longer perfect for it. You end up facing the possibility of hiring a new less-than-perfect candidate because you have already spent so much time cultivating a relationship with him or her.

Now you are asking yourself, if traditional talent pipelining wastes so much time, money, and talent, how exactly should you approach your recruiting? The answer may lie in Toyota's innovative idea; Just-In-Time recruiting.

With Just-In-Time recruiting, you don't waste any time building and maintaining relationships with candidates while there are no positions available. Instead, you only look for candidates in real time, when a specific position is open and instead of spending time building relationships with candidates who may never have anything to offer, you only look at the resumes "CV" and candidate profiles of people who fit the job. These people can be immediately identified as good matches for the position when it's needed, without you are spending time maintaining a relationship with them. You search for and contact candidates only in direct response to a hiring need.

In order to make Just-In-Time recruiting work for your organization, you will need access to a lot of resumes "CV" that can be available to you on-demand.

You can even link your system to social network profiles, for example via the LinkedIn Recruiter Platform, which features a talent pipeline solution in which you can upload information about candidates to be matched with the person's personal profile on LinkedIn and even if the candidate doesn't have a LinkedIn profile, it will save the information for you. With this system, you can count on information that is updated regularly, so you will know when a candidate has added something to his or her resume "CV" like another job description or a new skill.

Letting go of the traditional talent pipeline can be difficult. You may face an urge to maintain the status quo, but consider this: Just-In-Time recruiting can not only save you time and money, it can also help you find the one, the best candidate for the job at the right time, instead of settling for someone just because they were floating in your talent pool.

Chapter 8: Human Capital Supply Chain Management Recruiting

The process of identifying an organization's talent needs and identifying, acquiring, and retaining talent for those needs is essentially human capital supply chain management.

Just to remind ourselves again. A supply chain is a system of organizations, people, technology, activities, information and resources involved in moving something of value (a product, a service, or a person) from a source to a customer/consumer.

Conventional supply chain activities transform natural resources, raw materials and components into a finished product that is delivered to the end customer.

In recruiting, human capital supply chain activities transform relationships and data (ad responses, resumes, social networking profiles, etc.) into candidates that are delivered to hiring managers.

So why is it that there is quite a bit of resistance to applying proven supply chain management principles and practices to human resources and recruiting functions?

Let's take a look again at how Lean principles and Just-in-Time concepts can and should be applied to recruiting.

The main principles of the Toyota Production System are:
1. Continuous Improvement.
2. Respect for People.
3. Long-term philosophy.
4. The right process will produce the right results.
5. Add value to the organization by developing your people and partners.
6. Continuously solving root problems drives organizational learning.

Sound principles for any business or organization, yes?

The primary focus of Lean is creating more value with less work, and considers the expenditure of resources for any goal other than the creation of value for the end customers.

Would your customers (candidates, employees and hiring managers) have any issues with you focusing primarily on creating value for them? I didn't think so.

Activities that don't add value or are unproductive are wasteful (Muda is the Japanese term for waste).

Critical to effectively leveraging Lean is the identification of which steps in a process add value to customers and which do not. After classifying process activities into these two categories, the focus is to take steps to improve the former and eliminate the latter.

Having a good understanding of the hidden wastes inside of the recruiting process will aid in your appreciation of what Just-In-Time recruiting is designed to accomplish.

In Lean recruiting, anything that doesn't provide value to candidates, employees, and hiring managers is waste.

Chapter 9: Think Outside the Box

You often hear people complaining about recruiters and recruitment. Human Resources Departments, outsourced recruitment functions, and agencies are used to a series of common 'moans'. Emails disappearing into black holes, candidates' questions not being answered, people holding out on decisions or cancelling roles.

As you might imagine, this reputation is not indicative of Lean or Operations Excellence thinking.

What if these people were your customers?

Would you ignore their emails and queries, not tell them if you were shipping their product, or just cancel a product line without telling them?

Of course, you would not; because that would destroy your brand and business.

Well, they are your customers.

When you look at recruitment, the 'customer' is often deemed to be the client paying the fees, or the internal department which you are recruiting for. Which is of course correct; however, every single candidate that applies for your business is also a customer of yours; always metaphorically, sometimes literally.

For every thirty candidates that apply to Spring Raise Ltd, only one is successful. At each stage of the process we could ignore those who don't make it through, but we choose not to. We make sure we are courteous, we respond promptly, and where appropriate we provide feedback.

Apart from simply being good manners, we want people to advocate for us, not militate against.

If we dealt with a candidate badly, and they ended up in a leadership role where they were selecting a recruitment partner; guess who may not make the tender list? We realise that these scenarios don't often occur, but given the opportunity wouldn't you rather people have a good brand experience, rather than a terrible one?

Put yourself in the candidate's shoes. Aim for a brilliant employee at best and a brand advocate at worst.

1. Start with the candidate journey.

Make the process easy to understand, and intuitive, and don't waste their valuable time. That doesn't mean you can make it a difficult, selective process; but it does mean you should make it simple to navigate and clear to understand.

2. Consider the whole process.

Remember the candidate journey does not start when their CV lands in your inbox. Think holistically;

consider the end-to-end process. It starts when the candidate decides they are looking for a new role and crucially it doesn't end until they have completed their probationary period.

Be flexible, and use different channels; online application processes, out-of-hours interviews using Skype, etc. Remember these only work if they are joined up as part of the overall process.

3. Operations Oversight

Don't forget your basic operations management. Planning, improvement, and coaching are all vital parts of any process and as this is a process revolving solely around people, it is either brand damaging or brand enhancing.

4. Avoid failure demand

Make sure your recruitment team is truly adding value. Rework or 'failure demand' can make people look busy, but you will soon work out if they are spending time correcting mistakes from earlier in the process. Work out why this is, and keep the staff focused on the value chain.

5. Resource effectively

As in any process, capacity and demand will fluctuate; so they need to be managed. Understanding daily, weekly and monthly patterns can enable managers to achieve exacting service standards at the lowest possible cost.

Don't forget that people are the most important part of your business. They are your employees, they are your customers, they are influencers, and they are advocates. Treat them well, and treat them fairly.

Chapter 10: Tips to Improve Your Talent Acquisition

We recommend that you follow these recruiting tips to improve the productivity and effectiveness of your talent acquisition strategy.

1. Time is of the Essence - Make Sure Yours is Planned Wisely

Time management is a key factor in project management. Create a planning strategy that works for you. When you plan (whether it's at the beginning or end of the day) and how you plan (to-do lists, calendar blocks) is your prerogative. Just be sure to plan out both your week and your individual days to help you stay organized and on task.

At the end of each week, plan for the next week. Ask yourself, "What do I want to accomplish next week?" and, "How much time do I have to accomplish each task?" Then create a plan for yourself.

Example 1: "I am planning to focus on the Nurses search next week, and I will need eight hours to source, interview, and send candidates to the hiring manager.

Next, plan your day. Ask yourself the same questions, "What do I want to accomplish today?" and, "How much time do I have to accomplish this?" Then, create a plan for yourself.

Example 2: "Today, I will spend 6 hours on the Care Assistant search, 4 hours sourcing, and 2 hours for a scheduled phone interview.

Piece of advice: Stick to your plan. Sure, things come up and you need to be agile in order to accommodate changes, but having a written-out plan and knowing what comes next will help you stay focused and cut down on distractions.

2. Take Advantage of Social Media

Having a real-time social media presence is incredibly important to talent acquisition. Find out tips on how to develop a social presence for your recruitment function and how leveraging your employees' social networks to increase your reach in talent acquisition.

3. Set Timelines and Deadlines to Stop Wasting Time

Setting timelines and deadlines will significantly decrease the time you spend waiting, emailing, and calling back-and-forth to find out answers.

a. Ensure hiring managers and stakeholders involved in the interview process agree to a 48-hour timeline for feedback.
b. If a candidate is updating their resume "CV" and will get it back to you, set a specific timeline. Ask the question: "Can you have it to me by Friday?"
c. When you extend an offer, make sure you clarify a timeline for responding, as well. Let

the candidate know he or she has until a particular day and time to get back to you.
d. Instead of simply asking for availability when you schedule an interview ask whether the candidate is available at specific times and give a list of options that work for the interviewer.

Setting timelines and deadlines will reduce unnecessary email/phone and will give you specific times to know when it is okay to email/call/ask for what you need. When the deadline passes pick up the phone or shoot over an email. You will still experience delays and people will miss deadlines, but if you don't set them in the first place you are wasting your own time.

4. **Update and/or Implement Recruiting Metrics**

In order to take a data-driven approach to decision making, implement a system of recruitment metrics. Monitoring metrics and critical results will allow for greater productivity and effectiveness of your talent team.

5. **Share**

It's as simple as that. Create an environment that encourages sharing as a simple, yet effective, learning tool. Your team should share ideas, scenarios, industry news, recruitment articles, etc. Don't just share internally. Leverage and build your online presence by sharing these ideas through blogs.

Chapter 11: High Performing Talent Acquisition Function

It is no secret that talent is a key differentiator for businesses. Having the right people in your organization gives you the ability to out-innovate and outperform your competitors. The real secret is in finding, attracting and retaining these individuals. With competition for talent at an all-time high, you need a high-performing talent acquisition team that can consistently acquire the people your organization needs to succeed.

In this chapter we identified 12 dimensions of talent acquisition that high-performing organizations consistently exhibit. Each dimension has a role to play in a high-performing talent acquisition function, and together they drive lasting business results. For the sake of analysis, we divided these dimensions into two segments; **Strategic and Core**. Here they are, listed in no particular order.

Strategic encompasses elements such as business impact and workforce insights. These are capabilities that affect business performance as well as high-level talent acquisition outcomes.

1. Innovating to meet the demands of the business.
2. Providing strategic thinking to shape business decisions.

3. Demonstrating agility to meet changing demands.
4. Generating insights contrasting workforce needs with the market supply of talent.
5. Delivering quality hires consistently.
6. Measurably impacting major organizational initiatives.

Core includes the operational and process elements that support talent acquisition performance.

1. Communicating your employer value proposition.
2. Delivering great experiences for candidates and hiring managers.
3. Crafting a comprehensive strategy.
4. Simplifying recruiting processes.
5. Sharpening recruiting acumen.
6. Using recruiting analytics to inform business decisions.

Build your talent acquisition function to out-innovate and out-perform your competitors.

Unsurprisingly, organizations that performed well in these dimensions also excelled in their respective markets. Your talent acquisition team should focus on these areas to improve its ability to find and recruit the best talent; but it is unreasonable to think you can achieve excellence on every element all at once. Our belief; backed by research is that you should focus on core traits first in order to more effectively deliver on the strategic dimensions. You must have a solid foundation of core skills in place so that you do not sway in your attempts to innovate and deliver strategic recommendations.

There are room for improvement in core recruiting capabilities. Whether it is through additional training, partnering with expert providers, hiring experienced new team members or a combination of these things, the talent acquisition function must get back to the basics in order to succeed. Creating a rock-solid foundation of recruitment capabilities should be your top priority.

Chapter 12: Testing Cultural Fit During the Recruitment Process

As workplace structures evolve, finding candidates who are the right "cultural fit" is now a top priority of recruiters.

In business world (and in life), we tend to gravitate toward people similar to us. Our recruiting practices are no exception; if you are an introvert, you might find extroverted candidates off-putting. A detail-oriented recruiter might be uncomfortable recruiting an abstract thinker; however, seeking cultural fit doesn't mean recruiting clones. In fact, research shows that diverse teams actually perform better than like-minded ones. It is vital to be able to recognize a strong fit for your company, even when a candidate's personality and ideas might be far different from your own.

There is no denying that cultural fit is important but make sure you actually know what it is before judging candidates. It is easy to mistake cultural fit for personal biases; just because you would not mind being stuck in an airport with a candidate does not necessarily mean he is a great fit for your company.

A candidate's approach should not be so divisive that it creates rifts among employees, but you should not be afraid to hire somebody whose personality clashes with your own. If you perceive that a candidate would make a meaningful contribution to your company while maintaining decorum, that candidate might be a cultural match.

Here are four ways to determine whether a candidate might be a good fit for your company.

1. Differentiate between the person and the job

Your applicant is not interviewing to be your best friend; he is interviewing to be a great contributor to your company. Never lose sight of this during the interview. What you like about a candidate personally cannot trump his potential as an employee.

2. Have candidates take a personality assessment

A Personality Assessment can offer you concrete metrics by which to judge candidates for a particular position before they ever set foot in your office.

For instance, if your company wants to hire confident individuals with strong leadership skills and the ability to make objective decisions, you might take a close look at candidates' personality assessment results. The assessment can reveal whether somebody is an introvert or an extrovert, how he processes and interprets information and whether he makes decisions through logical reasoning or his intuition. Personality assessment provides a quantitative basis for making recruiting judgments based on personality.

3. Don't be afraid to ask off-the-wall questions

As long as you don't ask prohibited questions during the interview process, it is your prerogative to ask candidates about anything from their appreciation for football to their favourite foods.

Interviewees prepare for interviews by rehearsing boilerplate responses to conventional questions. Get a real impression of who they are as people by steering conversations toward unexpected topics. The ability to take the unexpected in stride is a plus, even if their hobbies and interests are different from your own.

4. Give applicants a chance to lead the conversation

We have all been to interviews where the interviewer sticks to an approved list of 10 questions and treats it as a strict Question and Answer session between the interviewer and interviewee. While this might be the most efficient way to churn through questions, it can only tell you so much about the person.

Instead, hand the interviewee the keys. See how he communicates without prompts or guides. This is certainly a greater challenge than offering a distinct question to answer, and it can provide an opportunity for vibrant personalities to shine. If interviewees have difficulty conversing with you of their own accord, that can be a sign that their personalities do not fit the position.

Cultural fit clearly plays a pivotal role in today's recruitment process, but that does not mean you should hire clones of your existing staff. Differing backgrounds lead to positive, productive innovations and exchanges of ideas. Once you truly understand your company's culture, make sure you are focused on it not your personal biases when vetting candidates.

Chapter 13: Recruiting for Fit Instead of Experience and Education

Do you recruit for fit?

Many companies say they do, but not all of them are executing it well. Here is a look at how and why you should recruit for fit, and why we think it trumps experience and education.

A recruiting-for-fit process gives you a competent candidate who is most likely to succeed, perform, and be most productive in your role. This delivers maximum value per recruitment and helps you avoid the high costs of mis-hiring and employee turnover. Cultural fit is associated with positive outcomes that include greater employee commitment, superior job performance, longevity with the organization, and greater job satisfaction.

Pre-definition is key to hiring for fit and match. It requires that you have:

1. Your company culture clearly articulated and agreed upon.
2. The characteristics necessary for success in this role spelled out.
3. Agreement from the team on the role and its characteristics.

One could ask why recruiting for fit over education and experience?

Experience and education are certainly important, but they are not the only thing you should be looking at above all others; when making a recruitment decision.

Here are four things employers need to know about fixating on education and experience at the expense of other candidate qualities.

1. The problem with relying on education

The smartest, most highly-educated candidate may not fill the necessary job functions best out of all your candidates, and they may not play as nicely with others. Pick the candidate best for your job, at your company, not the one with the most impressive degrees.

2. The problem with excluding candidates based on strict education and experience requirements

Often, employers will start out with an idea that the best person for their role should have a tightly-defined educational background or a certain number of years' worth of experience in a specific industry. The danger is that you will define away your perfect candidate. If you find someone who fits your "Who" to the letter, but they have experience in another industry, or a degree in a different field, or have not met your minimum years of experience, wouldn't you still want to meet them? Being overly conservative with your recruitment requirements limits your candidates pool. You are better off being able to consider, compare and contrast options from a rich pool of applicants.

3. The problem with relying on resumes "CV"

Resumes "CV" are marketing documents that present candidates' exaggerated versions of their education and experience. Beware the charms of a resume. Instead, get excited about the degree to which a candidate matches your "Who" and the requirements of your role.

4. What you need to know about education and experience "premiums"

Keep in mind that if you do find a candidate who is a perfect fit for your "Who" and also has a highly credentialed resume "CV", with strong education and experience, they are likely to command a high salary. On the other hand, a candidate who is a great fit for your "Who" but has a more average background can still offer strong potential to your company. Plus, they deliver greater value, as you are not paying a premium for first-class education and experience that you don't actually need. In fact, this "sweet spot" is where we recommend most companies to focus their recruitment.

Are your attempts to recruiting for fit missing the mark?

From experience this is a common problem; a company believes they are recruiting for fit; but actually "poor fit" is being used as an excuse when a candidate just doesn't "feel right."

How do you know if this applies to your company?

If you don't have:
    a. A tightly defined company culture; and
    b. Prior team agreement on the specific, defined qualities a successful hire would have in this role.

Then you cannot be rejecting candidates for poor fit and cultural mismatch; you have not even defined.

Recruiting for fit and match is not an excuse to pick favourites.

Employers in this situation who claim to be motivated by fit and match are likely to be making decisions based on gut instinct and personal affinity. Such recruitment methods still have a 50% chance of resulting in a mis-hire.

How does your recruitment process stack up? Are you well-positioned to make the "right-fit" recruitment your business needs to compete?

Food for Thought!

Chapter 14: Effective Small Business Recruitment

If things have been looking up at your organization, you may be eyeing a few new potential staff members as well. If you have been on the sidelines in the hiring game these past few years though, you might want to take a few moments to review some best practices for your expanding team. Here are seven tips for effective hiring at your small business.

1. Measure passion: Skills and talent are important, but you must also take into account whether candidates are passionate about going to work for you. Did they do pre-interview research to inform themselves about your organization? Are they enthusiastic during the interview? Do they illustrate their talents and passion with stories of previous experience? It is answers to these types of questions that can help evaluate whether or not potential employees really want to work for your company, or are simply looking for any old job.

2. Utilize established relationships: Often, you can find employees just by contacting folks you already have relationships with. Dial up some of your business colleagues or post an update on LinkedIn.

3. Offer incentives to team members: Your current staff represents a goldmine for finding new employees. Institute a referral program in which team members can earn cash rewards for referring a new hire.

4. Institute a "day in the life" program: Consider creating a program where potential hires come in and shadow one of your employees for a day. This familiarizes candidates with your day-to-day operations, plus it gives you an idea of how they function with your existing staff. If you are hiring freelancers or virtual employees, schedule a Skype meeting with a current staff member to discuss duties and responsibilities.

5. Search social media: When using social media to find candidates, LinkedIn should be your first stop. After that, check any potential hires for inappropriate Facebook postings, as well as negative or offensive tweets. Be sure that you do not factor any protected class information into your hiring decisions (gender, race, religion, age, disability, origin or pregnancy).

6. Interview like a pro: Whether in person or over the Internet, make sure you get the interview right. Show up on time, be positive, and diligently address any red flags you may have found on a resume "CV". There are good and bad answers to any issues; interruptions in work history, for example; so make sure you ask all the right questions and let candidates respond accordingly.

7. Consider hiring older employees: Older workers can bring a certain level of experience to your organization that younger bucks just don't have. Plus, if they work out, they can help mentor younger team members. They also tend to give better attention to detail and are typically more organized.

Now that we have talked a bit about best practices for hiring, let's discuss pay. If you are not willing to loosen up the purse strings a bit when an excellent candidate comes along, you may not improve your team's quality by much. If you are not familiar with average pay rates for the position you are hiring, check out your industry salary websites to ensure you offer fair compensation. Hiring the right folks for your small business is important, but paying them appropriately can keep them around for a long time.

Chapter 15: Big Business Recruitment Strategy

In my opinion you don't need a huge bank balance to compete for talent against giant corporations; however here are some ideas on Big Business Recruitment Strategy you should be copying.

In the pitched battle for smart, skilled recruits, you need to take every advantage you can get. But small and medium sized enterprises often don't have the sophisticated 'brand feel' that large, well-known firms use to distinguish themselves in the talent marketplace.

That is why it's so important to proactively work toward creating a cohesive brand voice and outward-facing profile that represents your company and culture in the best possible light. When done effectively, a well positioned, outward-facing profile can help you attract strong talent and give prospective employees a representative glimpse into your organization.

Building an outward-facing profile goes beyond simply describing your organization. The face you show potential recruits must exemplify your corporate culture and values, and get people excited about working for your business. Your recruitment positioning encompasses everything from your elevator pitch to your social media presence to the way you write job postings.

Here are three ways to build an outward-facing profile to attract the right talent.

1. **Communicate a mission and vision that people can identify with**

A major player in retail e-commerce mission stems from a personal anecdote about selling sports equipment to customers who loved sports as much as they do. The founders took it upon themselves to build the tools to facilitate their sales, and since then, they have been on a mission to improve e-commerce for everyone.

By telling this brief, personal story, this company not only established credibility as a savvy retailer, but also connected with their stakeholders in just a few short lines.

As a business, it is important to shape your communications with your audience in mind, and relating to them on a personal level is the best way to do that.

2. **Use your social channels to bring your values to life**

Thanks to social media, businesses now have a rich medium through which they can infuse life into their brand and live their values every day. Social media is an effective way to engage with customers, employees, and job seekers.

A large furniture retailer mission was to make the home a better place. It is a broad statement, and a perfect opportunity to exemplify what this really means through their social media channels. This company's Pinterest, Twitter and Facebook pages include great visuals and tips, while video blog posts provide engaging content featuring such characters as young couples looking to decorate their first home; who just happen to be their prime audience.

3. Speak to your target demographic

When it comes to searching for talent, speaking to your target demographic doesn't mean defining a target age group or demographic. Talent comes in a variety of forms, but an effective outward-facing profile draws in the right people.

Let's go back to the retail e-commerce company I mentioned earlier. Their profile speaks to people that are creative, value work-life balance, and are interested in personal growth within the firm. It does so in a few interesting ways; videos that feature cool problem-solving initiatives to emphasize the importance of critical thinking and learning; stats on average employee age (with the qualification that they want people looking to learn and grow, no matter what age); number of babies born to employees to emphasize the importance of work-life balance; and countries of origin to emphasize the importance of diversity of background and experience. Photos show an open concept office with shared spaces and a casual dress code. As a prospective employee, you have a very clear picture of the type of person that would thrive in this company's environment, and this is one of the keys to an effective profile.

Keep it simple. Write with your audience in mind, and be mindful of using corporate speak. You want to make sure you are sending a consistent message across all platforms to highlight your company culture clearly.

The process of building an outward-facing profile is a two-way street. Prospective employees want to envision themselves at your firm. You want your firm to be represented in the most precise and positive light possible to attract the right fit. Finding that elusive talent will allow you to spend less time recruiting, so you can spend more time growing your business.

Chapter 16: Ways to Attract Top Millennial Talent

As a vast number of tech-happy, smartphone-wielding millennials enter the job market every day, they are quickly superseding baby boomers as the largest group in the country's offices.

By 2030, millennials are expected to comprise almost 75% of the workforce, making it increasingly important for small businesses to effectively communicate with and understand this burgeoning pool of workers.

Here are four ways that small businesses can attract top millennial talent.

1. Moving to mobile

Small businesses with mobile-enabled websites will attract more millennial candidates than less digitally savvy competitors. Millennials are attracted to the convenience and ease of use that a mobile-enabled website offers. They want to receive job alerts, check on the progress of an application and look at additional job postings on their phones.

Employers can take advantage of this by providing web responsive case studies, infographics highlighting employee benefits, as well as video testimonials to further increase prospective employee engagement on their mobile sites.

2. Innovative workspaces

As exciting as the job description might be, millennials put a strong emphasis on the type of work environment they are being asked to spend their time in. You can't cater to their expectations with just mean a splash of new paint. Doing so requires a variety of seating options; couches, lounge spaces, and seats with a view as well as the flexibility for millennials to unplug with a provided laptop and work in their own homes.

Flexible working arrangement are already a major trend with tech and entertainment employers looking to attract top talent right out of school like Google and LinkedIn.

3. Ditch the old training manuals

Millennials recognize that career development requires more than a one-day training program, so small businesses should move away from the one-size-fits-all career development model.

The days of click-heavy computer-based training modules are gone. The appetite for traditional, classroom-based training is declining as the popularity of more innovative, interactive media formats rises. Videos, mobile apps, and online questions and answers are more in-line with the changing media consumption habits of a millennial workforce.

A company in the telecommunications space created a "Collaboration House," where employees can create an online presence or avatar and go to different virtual rooms for training. Users can interact with other employees, discuss training programs, and ask questions in these virtual rooms. It's a natural draw for millennials accustomed to entirely separate online worlds in the forms of social networks or massive multi-player online games (MMOGs).

4. Enhanced social presence

Social media is an indispensable tool in recruiting millennials, and a well-defined social media brand can help attract the best passive candidates.

A company in the insurance industry thought of themselves as social-averse two years ago. Now, thanks to a focused and committed effort to adapt to online recruiting, they are successfully using a variety of social media channels to find both passive and active job seekers.

If you are looking to attract and engage a millennial workforce, a comprehensive social recruiting strategy that links to your career page is imperative. In many ways, successful recruiting has become a marketing exercise, with a focus on the employer brand. To attract a millennial audience, build a presence on the social channels used by your target; designers and visually creative people may gravitate towards Pinterest, Vine and YouTube, while techies will find you via hashtags on Twitter and tech-focused discussion boards.

Millennials have already pushed the market to implement radical changes from product development, to marketing and beyond, disrupting traditional ways of doing business. Organizations that actively embrace these new strategies and examine their company culture stand to attract and retain a better-educated, more engaged workforce for future growth.

Chapter 17: Need for Speed in Recuitment is Increasing

In any job market; but perhaps never more than in today's workforce; top talent can come and go in the blink of an eye. Based on the pace needed to secure these top performers, you could make the assumption that the majority of companies are quick and poised to react quickly and efficiently to ensure they get available top talent.

But this isn't always the case; not all organizations wish to speed up hiring.

Some organizations believe that a longer recruitment process is helpful because it ensures that a company has adequate time to compare candidates and ensure that they are hiring the best person for the position. While there is some merit to this argument, it overlooks an important fact; recruitment must be equally viewed as both a people decision and a business decision.

Recruitment happens when a person is needed to fill a business requirement or gap. When recruiting an employee makes sense for the business, then it will happen. If not, then it won't. When examining the make-up of a company, it's not only important to examine all of the components that make a business successful and profitable, but to also understand how top talent is an integral part of that equation; a core part of its DNA.

Today, employees who were once reluctant to leave a job for fear of losing security are now more likely to make a move.

Furthermore, that pool of highly-qualified talent that was rendered jobless is more eager than ever to get back into the workforce. Now that opportunities are available particularly in sectors like healthcare and professional services where hiring is taking place, people are job searching.

If you look at data issued by the Bureau of Labour Statistics in the US, there is a significant difference in unemployment rates between those without a high school diploma and those with a bachelor's degree or higher.

Job searchers with a higher education face substantially lower unemployment rates than the national average.

As a result, there is a premium for these candidates and companies need to move quickly to ensure that the best of the best are working for you.

What all of this means is that just as there is a business reason to fill a position, there is a business benefit to filling that position quickly. A drawn-out recruitment process costs time and money that is too valuable to waste.

For everyday a company has not filled a position that solves a business problem, that company is losing money and, every minute spent on recruiting employees' costs money that could be better spent in other areas.

How to Speed Up Recruitment

Here are other ways which your organization can implement to speed up recruitment process:

1. Utilize your internal network. Your first step in the recruitment process is to notify existing employees of the open position. This may seem obvious, but sometimes it is a step that happens after the job has already been posted publicly.

2. Internal job postings give employees who may want to make a lateral move or change jobs within the company a chance to apply. They are also encouraged to look at their own professional networks for possible candidates.

3. Write a clear job description for the open position. This may seem like common sense. But, you would not believe how many times a candidate search goes awry because the hiring manager has not specified clearly enough the skills needed for the position.

4. Creating a thorough job description that helps Human Resources identify candidates in the first round will ultimately lead to better candidates and a faster recruitment process.

5. Be more selective about the candidates you bring in for an interview. The most time-consuming part of the interview process is often the first-round

interviews. Though many companies have a fairly rigorous screening process, including phone screens, too many bring in anywhere from 5 to 10 people for an interview when they may only be impressed by 3 to 5 of them from their resumes "CV".

6. Trust your gut in the resume "CV" review round to eliminate hours of potentially wasted time for you and the recruitment team.

7. Think ahead and eliminate steps that add time to your recruitment process. For example, many companies only ask for references once they have decided to offer a position to a candidate. If it takes a day or two for the prospective employee to get the references to you and then another day or two to contact those references, this can add up to a week to your recruitment process.

8. This can cost your company money in lost wages and administrative time. Request references from candidates at the time of the first round of interviews. Check the references for those candidates who make it to the second interviews before you think about extending a job offer.

9. Create a long-term talent plan. Most of the time spent during the hiring process is a result of seeking out qualified candidates to interview. Typically, the search begins when an organization has an open position. This means that your open position will take at least a month to fill.

10. To cut down time, hold informational interviews with prospective candidates for different areas within the company in advance of a job opening. This helps to build a pipeline of talent and can even eliminate the first-round Human Resources screening process that adds days and weeks to the recruitment process.

11. Ask for help or outsource portions of your recruitment process; whether you are a smaller company with a limited Human Resources staff or a large international organization working on recruiting multiple positions, the reason for a delayed recruitment process is probably largely out of your control.

12. Bringing in a Recruitment Agent in as a consultant to help with the recruitment process will cost money but save both time and administrative costs. You can also expect a quality screening and recruitment process from an outside consultant because you are paying for it.

The most significant benefit, when you speed up the recruitment process, is that the time saved allows Human Resources departments to pay attention to the initiatives and activities that will help you retain employees. It is easy to forget that retention and talent management are such an important part of the Human Resources function because recruiting can take up so much time.

As the skilled talent pool shrinks, companies must keep their eye on the prize. Ensuring that top talent is satisfied and engaged, so you don't risk losing your most valuable people, is imperative.

It is often said that the most valuable asset a company has is its people and I could not agree more. Getting high performing people hired and ready to work as quickly as possible is an important contributor to any company's success and a key to winning the talent game.

Chapter 18: Why Speed Matters in Recruitment

It pays to be thorough when you are evaluating a candidate, but you should be aware that the longer you deliberate, the higher the chance that you might lose the candidate to a competitor (most candidates apply to multiple jobs at the same time).

We all seem to be taking our time when it come to hiring decision; the average time-to-fill a job in the US or Europe has been on the rise over the last few years. Our research shows that the average is now roughly 25 days.

You might think that sounds like an appropriate amount of time to evaluate and hire the right candidate, but there is a problem. In many cases, the best candidates are off the market within 10 days.

Why does recruiting faster matter?

The very best candidates are in high demand and are likely to receive multiple offers. If you are not prepared to be decisive you may lose out to your competitors.

Recruiting faster doesn't mean you have to abandon your recruitment standards, but it does mean you have to move fast. This might mean you have to re-evaluate your process.

Here is why it's worth the extra work:

1. Higher quality hires

Moving fast means that you won't miss out on top talent. You still have to show candidates how awesome your company is though.

2. Better candidate experience

Being decisive with your recruitment process helps you differentiate yourself from competitors and improve your candidate experience.

You are not forcing applicants to continually return for interviews and wait patiently for feedback. Responding rapidly to talent and making fast recruitment decisions is so out of the ordinary that it's definitely something candidates will notice.

3. Higher acceptance rates

Reducing the time from interview to offer gives candidates less time to reconsider whether they want to join your company.

It also gives them less time to interview elsewhere or listen to counter offers from their current managers there is less chance they will get poached by someone else.

4. Your recruiters like it

Whereas a long recruitment process takes a good portion of recruiter's time; to schedule interviews and calls; hiring quickly helps them close requisitions, hit targets and stay happy.

5. Your hiring managers like it

Short recruitment cycles give hiring managers the talent they need immediately. It also helps them understand if they are causing delays in the recruitment process; correcting these can dramatically improve efficiency.

Chapter 19: The Process of Recruiting Faster

There are clear benefits to speeding up your recruitment, but making the necessary changes can feel like an intimidating task at first.

The key is to break it down into manageable changes that you can slowly implement.

Step 1: Planning

It is pretty likely that you will have to persuade your boss that changing the structure of your recruitment process is a good plan. Put together a pitch that demonstrates the potential Return on Investment "ROI" of speed. Argue that your organisation is missing out on great talent, and that a new approach could be a good way to change that.

The devil is always in the details. In order to speed up your recruitment you need to make sure that every element of the process has been carefully planned.

Make sure you agree on which interview questions to ask well in advance; don't just stick to the same old boring ones, try and think outside of the box.

Think about whether you need to meet each candidate face-to-face or whether you would be happy with a video interview. Not only is this far easier to arrange and eliminates many sticking points in the recruitment process, but there are some great tools out there that ensure you don't lose the personal element of a face-to-face interview.

Step 2: Inside out recruitment

The best place to start your search is always from within. Could anyone in your team handle the requirements of the role?

Internal hires tend to perform better and were likely to stay in their roles for much longer.

We often don't appreciate how valuable it is for workers to know the ropes of an organization. This understanding helps internal hires hit the ground running and perform from day one. It is also far quicker to hire from within.

Step 3: Test the approach

If no one from your team is a good fit it is time to look outside your organization.

After you have drawn up a new plan to accelerate your process, I would recommend testing it out on a small subset of positions you are recruiting for; if it is a success you can roll it out over the whole organization.

This policy should get support from any executives unsure of the validity of the idea, and will help you understand whether it can help you hire better talent.

Run a test with the faster approach on one of your harder-to-fill positions and see how your results compare. If it is clear that you are getting a better return on investment "ROI" then you should have sufficient evidence to convince your boss of the validity of a more streamlined recruitment approach.

Step 4: Build a consistent feedback loop

Even after you have seen the value that a faster recruitment process can bring you and your company, you need to keep testing and trying to improve it.

For every recruitment campaign you run, break down exactly what went well and what you could improve on. Use this data to establish a basic feedback loop.

This might sound technical, but all it's just an analysis of the effect of your 'actions'. This approach should help you understand which elements of your process need work and which are effective.

It might go against everything you have been told before but creating a faster recruitment process might be the secret to hiring the best candidates.

Chapter 20: Strategies to Attracting Passive Talents

The ability to attract passive candidates can be the difference between recruiting the very best talent in your industry and losing them to your competitors. There are various strategies brands can employ to attract and engage potential applicants; which often also prove more cost effective and successful than traditional recruitment methods.

1. Get involved in conversations online

Making efforts to remain connected and engaged with professionals on social networks helps to illustrate your brand's commitment to your industry and also build awareness, influence and perceived expertise.

Asking relevant and thoughtful questions to encourage feedback and discussion, helping others with their queries and generally getting involved in relevant forums will demonstrate that your brand makes time and is committed to helping educate and assist others as well as show an interest in their views. People want to work for a brand that is not only successful but also shows an active interest in their field.

2. Encourage employee referrals and advocacy

Enabling and encouraging employees contribute to your recruitment strategy is very effective in a number of ways. Not only are word-of-mouth and personal recommendations a very powerful form of marketing but they are also low cost too.

Employee referral programs help to encourage your workforce to spread your brand messaging and advocate a career at your company.

Ensuring that employees are engaged and treated well by the business will improve the likelihood of referrals occurring naturally as well as increasing productivity and happiness within the workforce.

A happy, openly engaged and enthusiastic employee will share their experiences of the brand culture and messaging with their social networks. If every employee has 100 friends and family members in their social circle then your potential talent pool is hugely increased.

Employees have 10 times more followers than their corporate social media accounts. (Source: Cisco)

Candidates referred to your business by friends or family are quicker to recruit than traditional candidates too.

It is faster and quicker to hire a candidate referred by a friend or family member, compared to candidate from a job posting or through a career site.

With relatively little time invested directly by the recruitment team to attract (other than administering referral/advocacy schemes etc) referred talent are also more cost effective to hire and will stay at your company longer, reducing turnover costs and building on employee expertise and advocacy.

3. Flex your expertise

Demonstrating your brand expertise and that of your employees will encourage talent who are looking to work for industry leaders. Those applicants that are searching for the next challenge to further their career will be seeking companies that demonstrate their expertise through the content they share and interaction with followers and peers.

Why work for a business that isn't seen as an expert in their field?

Influence and expertise can be increased and nurtured using a variety of strategies, such as:
    a. Writing guest posts and articles for industry blogs and magazines.
    b. Engaging in online discussions and forums.
    c. Partner with other industry experts.
    d. Provide speakers to industry events.

4. Follow and engage with your target talent

Once you have identified your target audience you can begin to target specific channels and even individuals as part of your recruitment strategy.

Answering relevant questions and offering advice helps to build influence and trust with talent and attract them to your brand.

Simply following certain individuals on social channels, such as Twitter and LinkedIn, will help to increase brand awareness and engagement. Following professionals will also help you to better understand their other interests which, in turn, will allow you to engage with them on other levels.

5. Maintain a useful and relevant company blog

Ensuring that you have a relevant and frequently updated company blog shows that you take an interest in industry news and trends.

Writing about and discussing topical stories will not only help you to stay up to date with what is happening in your sector but also helps to attract engagement from your audience and interest in future vacancies.

A company blog will also increase the number of web searches that lead to your brand online, increasing brand awareness and influence.

6. Be transparent

People are not interested in working for a business that offers no insight into what it is like to work as part of their team.

Sharing insider news and employee stories all help to illustrate what the culture is like and what a great place to work.

Honesty, openness and showing a fun and less formal view of life at your brand is key to portraying your company as an attractive proposition for passive (and active) talent. According to LinkedIn's Global Talent Trends report 66% of candidates care most about company culture, 54% about the perks offered and 50% consider the brand mission a priority.

Telling your story as a business will help to answer these questions and provide a clearer picture of your brand identity to potential applicants.

Regular updates from senior members of staff tell your brands stories from a different point of view and demonstrate participation and interest from all levels in the social side of the business.

7. Show purpose and passion

It is no longer the case that the salary associated with a role is the only element talent cares about. Purpose and fulfilment are top of the agenda for many individuals, whether actively seeking a new role or not.

By demonstrating WHY your brand does what it does you will help to attract applicants that are passionate and have a drive to achieve goals rather than simply getting a job to pay the bills.

Going the extra mile as an employer will help to illustrate passion and a drive to provide the very best service.

If you are hiring mediocre applicants that are not passionate about what they or their employer does then not only will that be reflected in your products and services but your culture will suffer as a result.

8. Think longer term

Hiring for the moment will limit your talent pool to those applicants available at that specific time as well as damage the quality of hire. Although there will always be certain vacancies that are unexpected and cannot be planned it's important to think long term and take the time strategise to hire the right people for the right roles as frequently as possible.

Giving yourself enough time to nurture passive talent will enable you to reach more individuals and target top talent without feeling rushed.

Recruitment efforts for roles that may not even be officially available can be running in the background, reducing administration for the Human Resources and Recruitment Departments when the need arises for those particular vacancies to be filled.

9. Talent attracts talent

Recruiting the right talent will help to increase and improve employee referrals and advocacy as well as building the right culture.

With the right talent working for you, it makes your employer brand that bit more attractive and may be the difference between you and the competition.

Studies show that engaged employees are 50% more productive and 33% more profitable. They are also responsible for 56% higher customer loyalty scores and correlated with 44% higher retention rates.

Quite often top talent will have a network of friends and acquaintances that would also be a great addition to your company whom they can refer.

10. Employer brand and talent brand wins

All of the above points are elements of maintaining a healthy employer brand. Treating your employees well and promoting what a great place your company is to work should never be forgotten or neglected.

If your employees are doing the recruitment for you then you are doing something right and you should make efforts to continue and improve on the formula. If they are not, then the likelihood is that things need to be improved in order to capitalise on the benefits that having a great employer/talent brand offer.

11. Get your job ads right

Making efforts to get your job ads right is key to a successful recruitment campaign. Most passive talent will need to be persuaded to take an interest in the vacancies you are advertising.

Simply listing duties and a brief description may well get you applicants but they probably won't be the ones who show passion and have been enticed even though they are successful in their existing role.

Illustrating some or all of the above points will help to build a great job advert that will draw the attention of top talent to your brand. Posting your advert in the right places will also help to target the right individuals. Using social media, both standard and sponsored, you can reach a large audience of relevant and passionate professionals.

12. Don't betray trust

If you betray the trust of those individuals that have made the decision to follow and engage with you then you will likely never be able to rebuild it. In order to gain and maintain the respect of passive candidates you need to demonstrate that your brand can be trusted and isn't adding their details to a sales database or similar.

Business updates are one form of communication that could bring tangible benefits to followers that have shown an interest in the business but these should be restricted to those that have proactively opted in to receive them.

If you are in any doubt as to whether your email will be considered spam then consider the following:
- a. The recipients requested it.
- b. The email arrives in a timely manner.
- c. The email is relevant to the needs of the recipient.
- d. The email allows the recipient to quickly grasp who sent it and what it's all about.
- e. The recipient can stop getting the emails easily and any time.

Chapter 21: Argument for Effective Employee Referral Program

Referral programs that produce competitive advantage incorporate exceptional features that make them highly effective. Those features are strategic, improve referral program quality, help sell the organization, improve the effectiveness of referral rewards, drive program responsiveness, and include strong communication and technology.

1. Strategic Features of Employee Referral Programs

The most effective employee referral programs incorporate strategic planning to get the desired results; top quality hires. Companies set up referral programs for success by focusing referral program resources on high-impact and hard-to-fill jobs rather than all jobs or jobs that can be filled with normal resources. When a high-impact position is vacant, focus the employee referral program marketing on it, offer varying awards weekly for referrals highlight the opening and keep it on employees' minds, and promote the referrer and new hire when the opening is filled. Pay attention to top referrers, those employees who have previous successfully referred good candidates, and give their referrals priority. Incorporate social media in your employee referral program to take advantage of the global reach it has created.

2. Improve Referral Program Quality

World class organizations with highly effective employee referral programs don't leave their referral programs in limbo or in the hands of an overburdened cross-departmental committee. They manage their programs to improve the quality and volume of referrals coming through their programs.

They do this by:

a. Targeting referral requests to the employees most likely to interact with the types of candidates needed instead of using a blanket approach.
b. Emphasizing diversity if diversity hires are desired.
c. Providing electronic or paper referral cards that praise the recipients.
d. Involving current employees who worked at competitors or other desirable firms that have the qualified candidates they seek.
e. Include non-employees in the referral program, such as retirees, vendors, spouses, and customers.
f. Conducting contact gathering events to encourage employees to review contacts and networks for referrals.

3. Help Sell the Organization

The best employee referral programs aren't just candidate sourcing machines. They are sales tools that tell the company's stories to attract and engage candidates. One of the best tools for this is compelling job descriptions. A compelling employee referral program slogan, such as Google's **"Good People Know Other Good People,"** gets referrers attention and interest. Giving top referrers the ability to guarantee an interview for their best referrals encourages them to really sell candidates on the company. Videos highlighting key employees, an exceptional work environment, current projects, or other key aspects of the company help engage and compel candidates to want to work at the company and take action to apply.

4. Improve the Effectiveness of Referral Rewards

Boring or inadequate employee referral program rewards just aren't part of best practices at world class companies. Advanced features of effective referral programs include improving rewards with several tactics:

a. Offer a charity donation option as a referral reward.
b. Offer prize drawings and other non-cash awards such as a reserved parking spot, lunch with the CEO, automobile leases, or tickets to high-profile events.
c. Adjust bonus amounts for different levels of referring and results, such as £50 for name only, more for full referral with resume "CV" and formal introduction and for top referrals that are not hired.
d. Offer bonus amounts for hard-to-fill or hot jobs.

e. Offer gross ups on bonuses, paying the taxes and giving referrers a full payout on rewards.
f. Handwritten thank you notes from the hiring manager or recruiter for the referral.

5. Drive Program Responsiveness

World class companies take employee referrals very seriously and give them the attention they deserve to ensure the responsiveness that secures quality hires. Responding to referrals within a day or two, interviewing "A" quality candidates within a week, and on-the-spot screening guarantee interest stays high and referrals don't get lost in the shuffle.

6. Include Strong Communication and Technology

Frequent and effective communication for the employee referral program processes are key to keeping referrals fresh and increase process awareness. Do this by including periodic feedback to referrers and candidates, holding follow-up meetings after top referrals, providing direct feedback about weak referrals, and opening a 24/7 help desk or help line for referral questions and guidance.

Technology for employee referral programs is important to success. Multiple channels for referring, such as email, web form, dedicated phone number, or text give referrers flexibility and help avoid missed opportunities. A website dedicated to the employee referral program that lets referrers track their referrals or stand alone referral kiosks for tracking and submissions also contribute to flexibility and ease of participation. Integration with social media such as LinkedIn and Twitter enables referrers to easily tap into their networks.

7. **Avoid These Referral Program Killers**

   a. Slow response to referrals and questions.
   b. Making referrers wait months to receive referral rewards.
   c. Using a blanket approach by asking all employees for referrals.
   d. Not tracking employee referrals in the application tracking system for analysis.
   e. Boring rewards or the same rewards for all referrals.
   f. Not giving feedback or direction on weak referrals.
   g. Too many rules and restrictions on referrals.
   h. Not giving referral applications and resumes priority in the recruiting process.
   i. Employee referral program manager turnover.

Take the advice of an experienced recruiting and hiring expert and give employee referrals the attention and resources needed for high quality, effective referrals of top candidates. Soon you will have the same kind of high volume and high quality referrals in your recruiting process as world class organizations who know the value of effective referrals.

Chapter 22: Guide to Building the Perfect Employee Referral Program

A top-flight employee referral program is a recruiter's best friend because, when they work well, the burden of recruiting no longer falls solely on talent acquisition.

It allows you to turn your entire workforce into recruiters. When you only have so many recruiters and so many resources to reach out to candidates, it helps to have a great referral program to empower all of your employees to help in sourcing.

It also helps the bottom line. Studies show referred candidates, if hired, stay at their jobs longer than traditional hires and a great referral program improves a business's overall retention rate.

Of course, all of that is contingent on building a strong employee referral program, as a weak one does little to help sourcing and a lot to hurt morale. Below are six-step guide on developing the perfect employee referral program.

Step 1: Determine the goal

The first step to creating any great referral program, like the first step of anything, is having a clear vision of what it should accomplish and it's not always just to get more referred candidates.

For example: A friend of mine said she is worked with some companies that have sought to improve their diversity via referrals, so they are looking for a select group of employees to refer more. Or, other companies want to increase referrals in specific areas of their company, such as sales, she said.

Once your team has agreed on the broad goal, it's time to get specific. For example, maybe right now 15 percent of your carers are referred candidates, and the goal is to get that up to 40 percent she said.

Step 2: Create an exceptionally user-friendly process

Okay, so now your goal is set for your referral program. The next step is actually creating it, which should adhere to the K.I.S.S. (keep it simple, stupid) philosophy.

The less work an employee has to do to refer a candidate, the more successful the program will be, The best-case scenario is that an employee just has to provide the recruiting team with a name and some way to contact the referred candidate, and the recruiting team takes over from there.

Quick story: Another friend of mine previously worked in talent acquisition at a large construction company that wanted its employees to refer more sales candidates. So, she built a program where all an employee has to do was get the business card of a great salesperson they ran into in their personal life;

such as someone who sold them a car, a watch, whatever and pass it along to her team.

Almost immediately, she began getting dozens of referrals for high-quality salespeople. The secret was just making it as easy as possible on the employees.

Step 3: Train your workforce

Okay, you have set up your referral program. Now it's time to get people to use it.

A good practice is to train your employees on how to use their referral program, and that training should cover three aspects:
 a. The practical nature of how to use the system.
 b. What your company is looking for in referred candidates.
 c. What employees can expect when they refer a candidate.

The first aspect is obvious; people need to know how to use your employee referral system. Hopefully, you followed the advice in step 2, and it is very easy to do.

The second aspect is teaching your employees what your company is looking for. While many of your employees might already know this, it is a good time to talk about what your leadership team values in a candidate.

The goal of this second aspect is to ensure your getting high-quality referrals from your employees; because, if your employees are constantly giving you people you have no interest in, it will create both more work for you and more frustration for them.

The third aspect is one of the most critical. The talent acquisition team needs to make clear what an employee can expect when they refer a candidate.

It is a best practice for each referred candidate to be contacted within a few days, even if it is with a rejection email. If this level of communication is impossible (and hopefully it isn't), then the talent acquisition team needs to set those expectations.

Say, in your program, a referred candidate will only hear from the company if they are deemed qualified enough to get an interview. While not a best practice, at least if employees know that ahead of time, they won't be as discouraged if they refer a candidate and the candidate never hears back from your company.

The single worst mistake a company can make with its referral program is to not contact referred candidates when an employee expects them to. If that happens, it's unlikely that employee will refer someone else.

Common question: What is the best way to conduct the training?

It depends on the size of the company. A smaller company might be able to have a 30-minute in-person company meeting to explain it, whereas a larger company will probably have to do something digital.

Either way, it should be relatively short, engaging and make both the process and the expectations clear.

Step 4: Continue to keep your employees engaged.

One of the biggest reasons employees don't refer more candidates is they don't know what jobs are open within the company. So, once you build your program and trained your workforce how to use it, it's time to put on your marketing hat and keep employees abreast of the open positions out there.

Again, there are systems out there you can buy that do this for you, but it's possible to do it manually as well. That can happen by sending out a weekly email with all open positions within your company or mentioning them during all-hands meetings.

Along those lines, most employees forget a lot of people in their networks, or are blind to the career advances and changes in their networks. To combat this, encourage your team to comb through their LinkedIn connections as a refresher and see if they know anyone who is right for your company.

Step 5: Recognize, recognize, recognize.

Your program's set up, you are reminding your employees about open positions and the referrals are starting to come in – congratulations! Now, it's time to share those kudos with the employees who are referring candidates.

The most common way companies do this is through money via a referral bonus, however, cash bonuses are not necessary, and even if you do give them, other forms of recognition are nice as well.

For example, a company leader giving a shout out to the employees who referred new hires during all-hands meetings is a great way to give recognition. Another is a sincere thank you from the talent acquisition team, either through email or in-person.

No matter what you do, doing something is important. An employee who refers a candidate and gets some positive recognition is likely to refer again, and it will inspire others to as well.

Step 6: Measure, measure, measure.

Always a critical part; measuring your efforts; these can depend upon your goal, but some good metrics to track are:

a. The overall percent of hires who came from referrals

The most common and most obvious statistic to measure is the percentage of new hires who were referred by an employee. There is no specific number to shoot for, just whatever the goal is that makes sense for your company.

If this number isn't as high as you did like, look to make it even easier for your employees to refer a candidate or do a better job of reminding your workforce of the open positions within your company. If both of those look good, then perhaps the problem lies within one of the following metrics.

    b. The percentage of referred candidates who hear from your company.

The goal here is 100%. But, again, it relates back to whatever expectations you set; if you said you did only contact referred candidates who were deemed good enough for an interview, have you at least contacted all these people?

If this percentage isn't meeting your expectations, you have to do one of two things; adjust your expectations or refocus on reaching out to referred candidates. If not, and your employees' referrals are not having the experience your team promised, the referrals will soon stop coming.

    c. The percentage of "qualified" referrals.

Essentially, this means the amount of referred candidates who are deemed qualified enough for an interview. This number should be (probably quite a bit) higher than the percentage of all applicants who get an interview.

If it isn't, it means your employees are referring the wrong people. To solve this, you may need to set clear expectations and standards for what your company is looking for.

d. Your workforce's participation rate in the referral program

All too often, a small percentage of a company's workforce is responsible for the vast majority of its referrals. If this number is low, it often means you need to do a better job of marketing your referral program and the open jobs within your company to your entire workforce.

e. The quality-of-hire of referred hires

Research suggests hires you get from referrals are of better quality than non-referred hires. That said, you have to measure it to ensure your employees are referring the right people.

Measuring quality-of-hire is always tricky, but you can use numbers like a new hire's tenure at your company or how well they do in performance reviews. Again, if this statistic is poor, it's worth training your employees on what types of people to refer.

Something to consider: Say you aren't getting the amount of referrals you did like, but you believe your program is easy for you employees to use and you are meeting the expectations your team set. Is it time to blow up the program?

Not quite. Other factors can have a dramatic effect on the amount of referrals you will receive. For example, if you just had major layoffs at your company, you will probably get fewer referrals. Or, if your team is really pushing to get a big project done, you will also get fewer referrals.

The good news is these can correct over time.

If you truly have a great program and yet you are consistently getting few referrals, it is a sign something is wrong within your company culture. After all, people will only refer their friends to companies if it's a good place to work.

So, at that time, perhaps more effort needs to go into making your company a great place to work, before you can start worrying about referrals.

All indications point to, employee referrals as one of the best ways to source candidates, as they get you better people, quicker. Simply put, a company that doesn't have a strong referral program is one that is missing out on a great opportunity.

Like most things in life though, an employee referral program is only as effective as its execution. By following the six-step guide above, you will ensure you get the most out of your program, which will alleviate a lot of the burden of your recruiting team and improve the overall talent within your company.

Chapter 23: Effective Engagement and Referral Tactics and Strategies

A critical link in the process of Lean/Just-In-Time recruiting is the conversion of candidates from their raw material form into in-process candidates. This involves successfully contacting and engaging potential candidates in 2-way communication. Having quick and easy access to a large talent pool is great, but if you are not very good at establishing 2 way communications with candidates you have not already established a relationship with, you are going to have a very hard time achieving Lean/Just-In-Time recruiting.

Remember that when tapping into large pools of human capital data, we are not targeting people based on their job search status; the goal is to find, contact, and engage anyone who is potentially well-qualified. Practically anyone can get an active or even casual job seeker to call them back or return their email; however, very few people are able to reliably get over 75% of people who are not looking at all to respond to an email or phone call.

The Bureau of Labour and Statistics estimates that 32% of all people are "passively looking" and that 34% are "not looking." That is fully 66% of the potential candidate pool and the portion of talent that most recruiters and employers covet the most! If you can't successfully connect with and quickly gain the interest of these people, you are at a significant disadvantage in achieving Lean/Just-In-Time recruiting (or any form of passive candidate recruiting, for that matter).

I honestly believe this may be one of the core reasons why traditional proactive candidate pipelining is used as a solution to meet hiring needs. If you can't get the majority of passive and non-job seekers who you have never contacted before to respond to you; your only option is to make the most of the people who you HAVE already contacted; however, being able to get practically anyone to respond to emails/call you back changes the game entirely; as you are no longer limited to the candidate inventory you happen to have on hand (your pipeline).

Having access to a decent volume of high quality human capital "raw material" via systems that are highly searchable is quite literally worthless without the ability to actually leverage the data and the search capability. The value of information is directly related to the ability to retrieve precisely the right information, exactly when you need it.

To achieve Lean/Just-In-Time recruiting, resourcers and recruiters don't have to be "Boolean Black Belts," but they must be proficient in candidate search best practices, techniques, and strategies. In order to retrieve information from information systems, it's critical to speak the "local language" and there is no getting around Boolean logic for querying data. Artificial Intelligence/Semantic Search applications and recommendation engines are great to have and can certainly help, but they are not a solution in and of themselves; they are not "the answer." Contrary to what some people may believe, Lean/Just-In-Time recruiting does leverage candidate pipelines; just not in the traditional way.

First, Lean/Just-In-Time recruiting involves the pipelining of raw material candidate inventory, in the form of resumes/candidate profiles. Recruiters and recruiting organizations should be proactively and reactively, manually and automatically building a database of potential talent on a continual basis everyday and night.

Unlike traditional candidate pipelining, when these resumes "CVs" are identified, acquired and permanently captured, the people that the resumes and social media profiles represent do not have to be contacted without an actual hiring need.

Second, Lean/Just-In-Time recruiting creates candidate pipelines as a result of sourcing and contacting potential candidates for a specific need. Any candidate that is not available, interested, or immediately qualified for the specific position being recruited for essentially becomes part of a work-in-process candidate pipeline.

This can be referred to as "reactive pipelining," and opposed to the "proactive pipelining" which involves contacting and engaging candidates without an actual hiring need.

Yes, I said the dreaded "reactive" word. I am well aware that many in the recruiting industry think "reactive" is a four-letter word; however, I am here to tell you that it most certainly is NOT. It's an 8 letter word.

Seriously though, it is a common misconception that proactive = good, reactive = bad. In reality, Lean best practices dictate that an ideal state of production is one in which a product is produced or a service performed directly in response to a customer need (pull).

Ultimately, building candidate pipelines as a result of Lean/Just-In-Time recruiting efforts is actually a mix of both reactive and proactive strategy. It is reactive in that people are contacted for a specific hiring need and proactive in that anyone not interested, available, or the right fit for the position being recruited for enters the candidate pipeline for future opportunities.

Some people seemed concerned that Lean/Just-In-Time recruiting was anti-relationship; that it might somehow endorse "forgetting" about great candidates you have spoken or met with.

Nothing could be further from the truth. No aspect of the Lean/Just-In-Time recruiting concept and strategy has anything to do with not building and maintaining relationships with great people. I just wanted to take a moment to clear that up.

While Lean/Just-In-Time recruiting supports building and maintaining relationships with candidates, it does not endorse doing so for no other purpose.

Remember that Just-In-Time is a Lean concept, and Lean is a production practice that considers the expenditure of resources for any goal other than the creation of value for the end customer.

Many recruiters who proactively build and maintain relationships with candidates for whom they do not have a current need, never provide any real value to the candidates. These recruiters proactively pipeline the candidates for their own personal benefit; to be able to have people they can quickly "activate," re-qualify, and submit when a position finally does open up; however, what real value is being provided to candidates who never move past the "relationship maintenance" phase in the recruiting lifecycle?

In a Lean/Just-In-Time recruiting scenario, candidates are not contacted prior to actual need; their time is not potentially wasted in a perpetual state of being "kept warm." If a candidate is contacted for a specific opportunity and it is determined that it is not a proper fit, or that they are not interested or available, they do enter the candidate pipeline for future opportunities and become work-in-process candidate inventory; however, in Lean/Just-In-Time recruiting, the level of "processing" (relationship maintenance) involved in being a pipelined candidate is typically lower than that of candidates who are proactively pipelined ahead of need. In Lean terminology, this means that Lean/Just-In-Time recruiting reduces waste (over-processing) and increases value for the candidates involved.

Here is a quick story to illustrate this point: A friend of mine was recruiting for an Area Manager with Care Industry experience and found someone with a very strong resume "CV" which was posted 7 months prior to the time she found it. She called him, left him a good message, and he called her back. He explained that he was not looking or available because he was working on a contract that was scheduled to end in 6 months. In about 10 minutes, she found out more about him and informed him of the kinds of positions she recruited for and typically had available. Then she asked if she could reach out to him in about 5 months. He said sure, so she set a reminder to call him in 5 months. She literally forgot about him until her reminder popped up 5 months later. She contacted him, qualified him some more, and submitted him to one of her clients. 2 phone calls, one submittal, one interview, one hire.

My point here is that she did not keep this person "warm" by chatting with him every 2-4 weeks during the 5 month period, and in no way to it prevent her from having a client hire a fantastic candidate who was extremely pleased with the opportunity. Minimal processing, maximum value for all involved; Lean/Just-In-Time recruiting at its purest form. She could have called this candidate every 30 days, but it would not have added any additional value to him or to her client.

In an effort to continually improve processes is critical to identify the assumptions and beliefs behind the current work process (i.e. "the way it's always been done") and to challenging them. Significant breakthroughs can be achieved when you are able to identify untapped opportunities through challenging and assumptions and traditional beliefs.

Do you really think the way that the majority of people and organizations currently execute sourcing and recruiting is absolutely perfect, offering no room for improvement?

I am trying to move the ball forward. I am not content with the way things have always been done. I do not blindly accept what others tell me, and neither should you. There is always a better way. What are you doing to find it?

I think that most people are trained on or learn about the concept of traditional candidate pipelining early in their careers, and I may be one of the few who was not. This seems to have given me somewhat of a unique perspective on the subject. In other words, no one ever told me the world was flat; that the most effective way to recruit has to involve traditional candidate pipelining.

What I learned largely through my own trial and error in the process of trying to not only keep my new job but also become the top performer for the company ended up being uncannily aligned with core Lean philosophy; creating more value for my candidates and clients with less work, and giving them exactly what they want, when they want it.

The expression "learning to see" comes from an ever developing ability to see waste where it was not perceived before. I did like you to try and work in a Lean approach to everything that you do; to view the expenditure of time and effort for any goal other than the creation of value for your candidates and clients/hiring managers.

I am not asking you to become a Lean/Just-In-Time recruiting convert; I am just asking you to think, and to examine your recruiting processes and practices with a critical eye for waste, such as unnecessary work in progress candidate inventory, over-processing, excessive waiting, overproduction, and defects.

Chapter 24: Conclusion

You might be familiar with our book Lean Startup that focuses on prioritising and launching your product as soon as possible and then analysing the results. So, why not do same for recruitment? Why not simplify the hiring process and test candidates before they officially join your team?

We discussed the concept of "lean", earlier in this book as whether it's related to Lean Manufacturing or Lean Startup, focuses on creating value for end users by reducing any unnecessary use of limited resources. One of the key components of the "lean" process is the rapid feedback loop, multiple iterations to quickly and constantly incorporate end users' feedback.

We agreed in this book that Lean Recruiting is based on this very principle where companies can create value (i.e. finding top talent) for end users (i.e. organisations, teams, divisions) by reducing any unnecessary use of limited resources (i.e. expensive and time consuming process of posting jobs, reviewing resumes and interviewing candidates). This can be done based on the rapid and multiple feedback loop (i.e. testing out candidates and getting quick feedback on their on-the-job performance).

The technology industry, from large enterprises to small startups, has been one of the fastest adopters of Lean and Agile in their product development process to launch quickly even though it may not be perfect, get feedback, iterate and improve. Yet, when it comes to recruiting talent, many tech companies still rely on the traditional method of recruiting; reviewing resumes and conducting a series of interviews which can often be a long drawn-out process. This is a form of inconsistency.

I believe that the Lean Recruiting model can be used in the following way, and in fact, I have seen more and more startups doing something similar to this in practice:
1. Quickly screen and weed out candidates that do not meet the minimum job requirements.
2. Bring in remaining candidates over the next 2 - 3 days and have them go through the job that they will be performing if they were to be hired. Set up the situation as close to real as possible.
3. Have your team members treat these candidates as if they are new members of the team during these days.
4. Collect feedback at the end of each day and share notes.
5. Bring in final candidates (select few) based on multiple days of feedback, have them perform the same job again for one day and make the final decision.

One of the most important aspects of this process is the feedback loop where the team that is in need of hiring talent is fully engaged during this process and can provide as much feedback as possible.

We discussed referrals in this book and stated that it take away a lot of the guess work during the recruiting process and can significantly reduce resources (time, money, etc.) for both employers and candidates. This is especially true if the source of referral is someone you can trust and respect. I see many new startups formed by the same ex-colleagues/teams who were tremendously successful before at other companies. I also often see and hear about many companies that some of their best hires are ones that have been referred by those people who care about what you are building.

We also look at how small business can hire the best people fast. In my view, defining who is "best" can be quite subjective. Yes, there are certain dimensions that make one candidate better than others. For example, it may be easier to identify who is the best iOS developer out there in terms of sheer engineering capabilities however, what if that person does not get along with the rest of the team? What if the person constantly looks for higher-paying opportunities? If so, that person may not be the "best" candidate for the team.

In Care Industry, especially at a company like Spring Raise Ltd; we look for talent that are highly capable, but more importantly, we value candidates who believe in our mission to change the way companies think about getting their immediate job needs filled while helping job seekers find such opportunities in the most frictionless way.

It is a long way of saying that to find the best talent, the team that is involved in the recruiting process should collectively do a great job in convincing the talent on the vision and create an environment where that person can be groomed to become the very best at the job as the team grows.

Remember if it doesn't Add Value – it's Waste!